RETHINKING MINISTRY ROLES FOR

Women
in
Christ

Books by Ray Barnett

The Gathering
Revelation (coming soon)

Booklets by Ray Barnett

Rethinking Ministry Roles for Women in Christ

RETHINKING MINISTRY ROLES FOR

Women
in
Christ

RAY BARNETT

Littleman Publishing

Littleman Publishing

www.littlemanbooks.com

info@littlemanbooks.com

First published, 2010

This booklet is an expansion of chapter 20 of the The Gathering, Littleman Publishing.

All Scripture quotations are from the HOLY BIBLE: NEW INTERNATIONAL VERSION®. Copyright © 1973, 1978, 1984 by International Bible Society.

Cover design: N Blythe

ISBN: 978-0-9807440-1-9

Library of Congress Cataloging-in-Publication Data

Barnett, Ray.
Rethinking ministry roles for women in Christ / Ray Barnett.
1st ed.
ISBN: 9780980744019 (pbk.)
1.Women clergy. 2. Christian leadership.
262.14

Contents

The night the rules were broken...

It was a large, conservative evangelical church. Women neither preached nor shared from behind the ornate, elevated pulpit. The carved chairs behind the communion table were reserved for men alone. It had always been this way. To act any differently would be an affront to the Word of God and the created order.

But one Sunday evening, a small woman mounted the steps and stood behind the pulpit. The pastor and deacons retreated and sat humbly as she began to speak.

For two hours she taught, challenged, rebuked and inspired the men and women who packed the auditorium to overflowing. And when she had finished, men and women walked out into the night, changed forever. Some became missionaries. Some entered theological training. Many, for the first time ever, began to understand what it really meant to trust and follow Christ.

What on earth went wrong? Had these most conservative of church leaders suddenly become feminists? Or liberals? Had they inexplicably denied the authority of Scripture for one night?

Or were they were compelled to admit that, beyond anything they had ever thought, taught or demanded, God had torn apart the foundations of their masculine superiority by the undeniable reality of what *he* had done in *his* kingdom through the preaching and teaching of this one, small woman?

More later, but first...

Why is it an issue?

I t's in the Bible!

> I do not permit a woman to teach or have authority over a man. (1 Timothy 2:12)

There you have it — a plain, unambiguous statement in black and white.

Or is it?

Why is that when Scripture seems to speak so plainly, there can be men and women who fully respect the authority of God's word and yet who champion the cause of women using their teaching gifts as freely as men? Are they trying to get around something they don't like? Are they just "women's libbers" or "feminists"? Or are they seeing things that might not be as visible on the surface of our English translations as our inherited perspectives suggest?

For example, it is interesting to note that the words "woman" and "man" in that English translation of 1 Timothy 2:12 (above) are Greek words *commonly* translated as "wife" and "husband" throughout the New Testament...over 50 times.[1]

Paul himself uses those exact same Greek words in Ephesians 5, where he says, "*Husbands* love your *wives*... *Wives* submit yourselves

---

1   Strongs Concordance has them: "gune - a woman; specially, a wife"; and "aner - a man (properly as an individual male): fellow, husband, man, sir." If you check those words in Strongs, you will see their varied translations throughout the NT as wife/husband and woman/man.

to your *husbands...*" And there is probably not an evangelical Christian among us who would imagine those words to mean anything other than husband and wife. Any other translation just wouldn't work. Nor would it in 1 Peter 3:1-7 when Peter tells believing wives how to win their unsaved husbands, and husbands how to live considerately with their wives.

Later, in the letter of 1 Timothy, Paul instructs Timothy that an overseer (church leader) must be "the husband of one wife". Here again, *exactly* the same Greek words. And in that place, who among us would imagine them to mean anything but "husband" and "wife"?

A serious possibility

Therefore, is it *possible* that in 1 Timothy 2:12 Paul wasn't talking about preaching or church leadership at all, but was talking about relationships within families? Might it be *possible* that what Paul said to Timothy in 1 Timothy 2:12 was simply a statement in keeping with what he said to the Ephesians and Colossians concerning the roles of husbands and wives within the family?

Yes, it is very definitely possible. And it is possible without any interpretative gymnastics or strained attempts to "get around" what seems (in English) to be so plain and simple.

So how do we decide whether the words should be translated "man and woman" or "husband and wife"? Where a genuine choice of translation is possible, how do translators decide which words to choose?

The real questions is: What did Timothy himself understand?

Clearly we will need to come back to 1 Timothy 2 and think seriously about the text, but before we do, there is a wide range of background issues we need to think about. The first and most foundational of all will be the affect of the Gospel on women.

3

The Gospel and women

The place to start is the Gospel! The subject of what women can and cannot do in church life will never ultimately be resolved by a finely honed grammatical argument. If a subject as important as the ministry of fifty percent (or more) of the entire population of believers is to be solved by a grammatical argument arising from two or three words in one Greek sentence, it will be a very weak solution indeed.

The *foundation* and *benchmark* of any understanding of the roles and opportunities available to both men and women will be the Gospel. All textual argument or interpretation must be able to be resolved within the framework of the Gospel – or what God has accomplished in His action of redeeming women as well as men. Our interpretations must honour the Gospel at every point. Even our appeal to male-female roles in Genesis and creation must be an appeal made through the Gospel, because our reconnection to God's original intent can only be through Christ.

What does redemption mean for women?

It is of utmost importance, therefore, that we be able to articulate a view of what redemption means for women. Men readily accept for themselves that redemption grants them freedom from all of the prohibitions that came as a result of the Fall. Having once been cast out of the presence of God, men once again have free and open access to God. Indeed, men have *boldness* of approach to Him despite their original and ongoing sins. They have the ability and authority to interpret and speak out God's word as a prophetic voice in the community and among the

4

Lord's people. As men we are unrestricted, uninhibited, and unashamed of who we now are because we have been set free from all that we were in Adam. Crucified, buried and raised with Christ so that "we too might walk in newness of life"[2], we gladly embrace the truth that, in Christ, actions and access once forbidden to all but the specially anointed few, are now open to every new-born man. Redemption for the man has been complete.

The serious question is: What does Redemption mean for women? Is *their* redemption also complete?

On the subject of reconnection to God and the ability to be His mouthpiece, here is the promise:

> In the last days, God says, I will pour out my Spirit on all people. Your sons *and daughters* will prophesy, your young men will see visions, your old men will dream dreams. Even on my servants, *both men and women*, I will pour out my Spirit in those days, and *they* will prophesy. (Acts 2:16-18) (Emphasis mine)

At Pentecost, God established a new regime that would countermand all previous social order, all privilege, all age exclusions, all race exclusions, and all gender exclusions. As Paul later says, "In Christ there is no Jew or Greek, slave or free, male or female." (Galatians 3:26-29) Now before we jump to the traditional retort that in Galatians Paul is speaking about salvation, remember that salvation is a package. To be in Christ means we also have the Spirit of God (e.g. Romans 8:9), and, as we see in Acts (above), to have the Spirit means to be reconnected to the process of receiving from God and speaking for God through the motivations of the Spirit of God. Old and young, male and female, will have the Spirit poured upon them, and they will prophesy because they have been reconnected to true wisdom through Christ who is Himself the wisdom of God.

If that is the promise, then applying a gag to fifty percent of believers perhaps needs some very serious reconsideration.

---

2   Romans 6:1-14

At this stage, it may be helpful to define prophecy. 1 Corinthians 14:3,4 gives us a definition, or at least a description, of the function:

> Everyone who prophesies speaks to men for their strengthening, encouragement and comfort... he who prophesies edifies the church.

So, prophecy is the act of speaking to encourage and strengthen the church. In 1 Corinthians 11, Paul has already told us that prophecy is a function open to women. That is in complete agreement with the promise quoted in Acts – it is a role equally open to young women and older women, not just to men. It is not a promise limited to one particular day – Pentecost – but was available to Corinthian women.

Assuming our definition of prophecy (from 1 Corinthians 14, above) is correct, the role of prophesying is a function that speaks to the church, because it edifies the whole church. Simply put – God is not unhappy with women speaking to build up and encourage and comfort the church because it is one of the miraculous fruits of the Gospel. The Spirit is for all; not just for a priestly caste or male gender. Paul also stated in 1 Corinthians chapter 14 that "all" could prophesy in the church meetings, one by one, and because that statement follows chapter 11, it cannot be seen as a freedom restricted to fifty percent of the church.

A Gospel issue

What we see is that, if we remove the tensions of the gender issue from centre stage and place the Gospel on centre stage, these freedoms described in Scripture do make a warm-hearted connection with what Christ has achieved. Men and women are reconnected to the wisdom of God and can speak His wisdom to each other because of what God has done in Christ. God has brought all social classes, all races, and both genders to the same place, filling them with His Spirit and reconnecting them to His wisdom. Gentiles and Jews, slaves and free, males and females can prophesy, that is, speak for the strengthening, encouragement and comfort of the people of God. To the Jewish mind that was shocking! (Perhaps to many western evangelical minds as well.)

To think any other way leaves us with serious questions about the Gospel. "Sin entered the world through one man, Adam, and death through sin…" (Romans 5:12) We affirm with all our hearts that men are fully redeemed from that foundational act through which all of creation was locked into a cycle of death and destruction, and all mankind was forever alienated from God and the indwelling of His Spirit. Men are fully redeemed from Adam's sin. They are reconciled to God, to each other, and to their women.

And women? To say that women are redeemed from everything *except* the deception of Eve, appears to leave us with a lopsided Gospel. For the man, Christ could remove all relational consequences of Adam's sin, but for the woman, Christ removed all consequences *except* that she is unable to speak of Christ to, or share her wisdom with, or use her vocal spiritual gifts in the presence of, fifty percent of the population of the church. (And some go so far as to suggest that her silence must extend beyond the church, unable even to speak of Christ or teach the Gospel to unbelievers.)

This is not the final argument, for we do need to look at specific texts, family order and so on, but please recognise this as the reason why, for some interpreters of Scripture, there appears to be a need to re-address those specific proof texts. For many people, the limitation of women offends their sense of the Gospel. It is not just a limitation placed on women, but is perceived to be a real offence against the Gospel and the adequacies of redemption. The silencing of women suggests that the Gospel has not fully worked for fifty percent of all saved people.

So it is not just a matter of "liberalism" or a broadside attack on the Church by rampant feminism. This is not a matter of war or an issue for fear and name-calling. Rather, we need to recognise that many of those who want women to be free to speak, want it for the highest possible motive – to see women receive a complete and equal redemption. It may even be that the greater responsibility rests with the more traditional view; their responsibility being to explain why it is that the Gospel does not work equally for women.

This is not a game of twisting logic, it is indeed a very serious question for us all. What does redemption mean for women? From what and to what have women been set free in Christ?

A return to the created order

The answer to the question at the end of the previous section may well be that women are set free to return to the original created order. With that I agree. However, we need to be very clear about what the created order really was.

The helper

In the beginning, the woman was made as a helper to the man. This does not mean that the woman was made *inferior* to the man. Nor was she made as the *servant* of the man. Only male bigotry could read the text that way!

That same Hebrew word "helper" is used of God in statements like, "The Lord is my *helper*". When we read this, none of us think of God as an inferior, submissive servant. To know that God is our helper, in no way detracts from our understanding that God is our infinite superior.

In the beginning, the woman was made complementary to the man. She completed and complemented him. As his helper, she was different but not inferior; she was in every way his "other half". Indeed, in Genesis the word "Adam" or "man" is used to describe *both* the man and the woman. Genesis 5:1: "And when they were created, he called *them* man." The Hebrew word for man is Adam.

God's view of the helper

Any reasonable examination of Proverbs 31 will show God's perspective on women - manager, in charge of staff, businesswoman, real estate developer, importer… Is it too obvious to point out that many of those tasks involve engaging with, mentoring and taking authority over men? Therefore a *general* prohibition on women doing such things, as some impose, is not possible to sustain in Scripture. What we see is a strong, intellectually capable human being exercising the abilities God had given her.

What are we returning to in Christ?

As we have seen above, the original created order was not that all women were to be the silent, acquiescent servants of all men. It was not that women were provided for the sole purpose of sex and procreation. It was not that Eve was to stand behind the man with a fig leaf covering her head when Adam walked and talked with God in the garden. The woman was not inferior. She was in every way "Man" – "bone of my bone, flesh of my flesh", the completion of the incomplete. Yes, she came from the man, but now that the Gospel has come, Paul has to point out the obvious to the Corinthians:

> *In the Lord*, however, woman is not independent of man, nor is man independent of woman. For as woman came from man, so also man is born of woman. But everything comes from God. (1 Cor 11:11,12)

In Christ, independence has gone and men have once again come to the point of recognising their dependence upon women.

It is worth noting that, with this argument in 1 Corinthians 11, Paul overturns the need for women in every major non-Christian religion to demonstrate their inferiority and submission to men by having a veil on their heads. In Christ, God returns Adam and Eve to the beginning, and as Paul goes on to say of the woman, her "long hair is given to her as a covering". Literally, "as a veil". That verse is the only place in the passage where Paul actually uses the Greek word for a material veil, and he does so in order to say that "in the Lord" the artificial (the material veil) has been replaced by the original – her *hair*. Even in this, women have been set free. Even nature – the created order – teaches this, says

Paul. As believers, we are not to look or act like a christianised version of Islam or Hinduism; our women are free and equal.

So in saying that the man and the woman return to the created order, make sure that it is the true created order, not the order of the Fall. The Fall was not creation, it was destruction, and the Gospel is not a perpetuation of destruction, it is a new creation.

Understanding what happened at the Fall

In approaching the subject of women, the Fall is not just a theological issue, it is a personal issue – you and I have been affected deeply and *personally* by the Fall! We will all view issues from a point of prejudice as a direct result of what happened at that catastrophic moment of sin.

At the Fall, a dramatic change took place in all created relationships – between humans and the earth, humans and the animals, humans and nature, and of course, between men and women. As a consequence of sin, the man-woman relationship would become a struggle for supremacy in which the man would win. The woman's desire would be to rule over her husband, however, the man would win, and would rule over her. Genesis 3:16 – the word for "desire" is the same word used of sin "desiring" to master Cain in chapter 4. The suggestion is not necessarily that of sexual desire, but implies the desire to gain the ascendency over, or to dominate. The woman would want to dominate the man but would lose.

This is important because, historically, most of the interpreting of the Bible has been done by men, and on this subject, as any other subject, men will be inclined to rule over women as a result of their fallen mindset. We need to admit that even our sincere, yet masculine, interpretations *may* have an insidious, underlying desire for domination.

Men need to recognise that the man ruling over the woman
- is *not* a blessing, it is a curse.
- is *not* what was meant to be; it was what came about as a result of sin and the Fall.
- is *not* a fruit of creation; it is an innate and lingering consequence of sin.

- is *not* a demonstration of wholeness but a proof of us being broken people in a broken world.

In far too many cultures, to one degree or another, *fallen* men control, boss about, emotionally brutalise, physically brutalise, socially and intellectually confine, limit, subjugate, relegate and dominate women. It is not what we were created to do, it is what we "fell" into. That consequence of our primeval history will affect men as they come to read and interpret scripture. Even as men renewed in Christ, it will be difficult for us to read the various passages on the roles of men and women free from those innate desires they had in fallen Adam. (Perhaps that is why, on the subject of marriage, God seems to say so much more to men than to women; men have much more unlearning to do.)

Before men can openly understand the text, they need to ask God for cleansing of this innate propensity, for it is strong and still dominates. In this area of male–female relationships, as in any other area of life, we are to be "transformed by the renewing of our minds." (Romans 12:2) Or, as Paul says in Colossians 3:10, we are to be "renewed after the image of our creator".

Women also approach these issues with fallen propensities. The innate desire of women can be to dominate the man. Some of the most "submissive" wives can be the most dominant, bullying by emotional blackmail or wearing down by constant verbal harassment or the man's fear of humiliation. The innate desire to dominate may well be there; however, it is often far less noticeable and is also often suppressed beyond recognition for the simple reason that in the contest between the sexes, the man wins – at least publicly. That is exactly what God said would happen.

Some of the broader issues

Understanding the setting

A nother issue we need to address is the setting into which the various gender-teaching instructions were originally written. There is no doubt that when we think of women speaking, we have a seriously distorted cultural picture. This misunderstanding adds dramatically to the tensions associated with the discussion.

Our mental picture is

women speaking = women preachers

women preachers = women standing dictatorially behind a wooden box, in an auditorium with a hundred silent, non-participative, listeners.

No honest reader of Scripture could even begin to imagine that this is the setting of a New Testament meeting. (If you do believe our auditorium preaching meetings are the way the early church met, you would do well to test those assumptions against the patterns and priorities of meeting as revealed in Scripture.)

Our pulpit-dominated setting is *not* the setting or culture of meeting into which Paul wrote his instructions. The early church meetings were not auditorium-based, nor were the attendees passive listeners to the one gifted orator. That may have happened at times but was not the usual setting for regular early church meetings. They met in homes and often met around a meal. In that intimate, home-based setting, their meetings were discussions of truth in which numbers of those present could speak, ask questions and contribute in various ways. So having a woman prophesy, that is, to speak so as to encourage, build up, and strengthen those present as permitted in 1 Corinthians 11, was not an elevated, titled, authoritarian role. It was a simple contribution to the lives of her fellow believers as she shared her wisdom. Understanding that as the original setting greatly diffuses the issue.

Today, in many churches, women are welcome to contribute to a Bible study group and to talk of the Lord at the dinner table even when their husbands and male friends are present. There is little or no tension associated with it. We adapt to the setting, and the setting diffuses the issue. Most would deem it cultic to have women keep silent at all times, even around the dinner table, when family and friends are talking about the Lord. But put women into *our* church setting – an auditorium, an elevated pulpit, sacred titles and the mystique of professionalism – and there is enormous tension.

Get the setting right, and we are much closer to getting the answers right. Conversely, the further we move away from God's original setting and style for a church meeting, the more complex and tense the issue becomes. In our setting and structure, the questions reach ridiculous proportions:

Should women be ordained to the priesthood? What a strange question for anyone who has even a passing familiarity with what God says about life and leadership in a local church. The real question should be: Is it proper for *men* be ordained to the priesthood? And the answer from Scripture will easily be, "No".

Should women be ordained as reverends? What a strange question for anyone who has read what Jesus said in Matthew 23:1-12. The real question should be: Is it proper for *men* to be ordained and called reverends? And if Jesus is to be taken seriously, the answer is easily "No".[3]

---

3   "Reverend" means "one to be revered". For a man to describe himself this way is a serious departure from what Jesus said. Think of Paul's angry outburst to the Corinthians, "What is Apollos?

The point is simple: Get the setting right and you may well find that even though there are differences of opinion on the finer application of certain texts, almost all of the *tension* diffuses because it becomes a simple and amicable discussion of propriety, not a major issue on which to divide churches and whole denominations.

Understanding the relationship boundary

As we interpret the truth of Scripture, we need to make sure that we keep within the boundaries of the original subject and intention of the writer.

While our perspectives on what submission means may differ, one thing needs to be clarified in our thinking: just who is the woman to submit to? The answer is that wives are to submit themselves to their husbands. That is the biblical boundary.

All women were not created to be the helper of all men! All women don't complete all men as "bone of their bone and flesh of their flesh!" The one woman was to be the helper of her *own* one-flesh partner. There can be no concept of the caste-submission of all women to all men. Any caste system - that is, privilege by birth, with all members of the one caste permitted to dominate all members of the other caste - may be comfortable for Hinduism but is not a Biblical concept between men and women. That all men feel they should dominate, control, or be in charge of all women is direct sociological evidence of the Fall and the curse, not an evidence of the created order as it was intended to be.

My wife is not to be in submission to all the men in the church. She is one-flesh only with me and completes only my life.[4] Nor are other wives in submission to me. I cannot begin to give them directions that they must obey (if that is your definition of submission)[5] just because they are women and I am a man. What right do I have to enter another one-flesh relationship on an equal basis with the husband in *any* area of that relationship? None whatsoever!

What is Paul? Only servants..." As Jesus said, "Don't be called [anything] for you are all brothers." Men, please let's recognise how easily we make rules for the women while ignoring the plain and easy rules that might apply to us.

4   Ephesians 5:22 "Wives submit yourselves to your husbands . . .'
5   And I am not actually suggesting that as the correct functioning definition of submission.

My wife does not submit to all men in the church any more than I am supposed to love all women in the church as Christ loved the Church. These things concern one unique relationship – that between my wife and me.

This will become very important as we begin to think about women remaining silent and "learning in submission" because the question must be asked at that point as well: In submission to whom? We must keep the focus of family issues in the family, church issues in the church and social issues in society.

Understanding the boundaries of the writers' intentions

The other major boundary is that of the people targeted by the Scriptural directives. Whatever we make of instructions about women teaching or having authority, they are instructions for the people of God. It is important to note this, because there are some today who teach that women should never have a teaching role in relation to any post-pubescent male. That precludes women from teaching religious instruction in schools. Some go so far as to say that a woman should not even teach maths and science to any male above adolescence.

However, the original setting gives us the boundaries for the instruction.[6] Paul wrote to Timothy about serious problems in the church in Ephesus. His letter was not a general note for Timothy concerning all social relationships across the whole city of Ephesus. Teaching and authority . . . these were issues being addressed *within* the Body of Christ. Therefore whatever we make of those instructions we must keep them in their place. To project them beyond that and make our view apply to women schoolteachers, women lawyers, magistrates and so on is going outside the legitimate subject of the passages concerned. Once we head down that pathway it never, ever ends. [7]

---

6 The problem is one of extended applications. When writers address a subject, we need to work with their intentions. An example might be the instruction of Paul to the Corinthians not to take a brother to court. Paul does not say we are never to take anyone to court. While that may or may not be covered by other writers in other places, Paul's instruction is limited to relationships within the Body. Anything beyond that is an extended application, and is illegitimate unless supported by other Scripture.

7 As noted above, this line of thinking has been pressed to distressing proportions by sincere

In the passages that comment on teaching, silence and learning, our New Testament is not reforming a universal social order but a marriage order, or a church order, (or both) depending on the passage. Deborah *can* judge Israel because she is not married to all the men in Israel.

Understanding our limitations

We like to be bold and definite . . . when it suits us. But sooner or later our limitations catch up with us and we begin saying what a passage meant to say, or what we would like it to mean, quite apart from its plain words. This happens when a passage just does not seem to match our own (predetermined) views, or is simply impossible to apply with any form of justice. What happens is that we reach the limitation of our understanding of the setting and the intent of the original text.

Later we will come back to 1 Timothy 2, a passage at the centre of the tension over women teaching and having authority. Some say it must be read as it is and applied as it is, plainly and without compromise. In fact, to some, any contrary action, such as having women preachers or Bible study leaders, is elevated to such an enormous level of significance that you would think it to be a one of the most powerful fundamentals of the word of God, established on almost every page of Scripture. People will walk out of a church, will fight a denomination, or will use insulting terms like "liberal" in the presence of any offence against what they consider to be such a direct statement of Scripture. And yet discussions about what Jesus said concerning male, Pharisaic leadership (Matthew 23:1-12) are very rare indeed.

It is a matter of serious inconsistency. Consider: Later in 1 Timothy, Paul *orders* the enrolling of widows on a list for charitable help. He *forbids* any such help to any widow under the age of sixty, and then *only* if she has lived an exemplary life. In other words, taking it literally, a widow who has lived a sinful life and has only just been saved will not be cared for by the church because she has no track record of piety. And even

---

but misguided evangelical men and women, to the point where women are not supposed to work in any way outside the home, nor have any position of authority over any post-pubescent male. I would again refer you to Proverbs 31.

if she is a paralytic in a wheelchair, if she is under the age of sixty she *cannot* be helped by the church. There are *no* exceptions given by Paul whatsoever.

Paul then says plainly that *any* young widow who decides to remarry brings judgement upon herself. (1 Timothy 5:9-13) Almost immediately after that, having just told them they come under judgement if they marry, he advises those same young widows *to* marry. In the middle he tells us that *all* young widows become idle gossips.

That is the "plain teaching" of Scripture in paragraphs in close proximity to the sentence about women not teaching men. It is what it says "in black and white." But we don't apply those things in "black and white." We don't have a widows' roll, we don't callously exclude widows under the age of sixty from all forms of material help, and we certainly don't demand a works-based (show us your track record) approach to the receiving of help when widows are hungry. Nor are there books and conferences and divisions and name-calling over these issues.[8]

Why? Because we recognise that a "black and white" application doesn't work! Somehow it offends us and our understanding of the grace and compassion we find inherent in the Gospel. We find we are compelled to make allowances for what seem to us to be "the plain words of Scripture" (or in most churches, we simply ignore them.) We are compelled to admit that where Timothy lived, there must have been something going on that we are not told about. It *seems* like an order of widows had been established, women who as widows devoted themselves to remain single and to serve the Lord. It *seems* that, in return, their needs were supplied by the church. It *seems* like they made a vow of single-minded service that younger widows were apt to break by wanting to remarry, and so it was better for those young widows to marry and not join the order of widows. That now makes sense and fits the grace and mercy we see in the Gospel.

We are not specifically told about any order of widows, but we are compelled to work it out in order to satisfy the sense of justice inherent

---

8   Perhaps this is further evidence that the heat of the "women teaching men" issue does not come from Scripture but from the innate desires of "fallen" men.

in the Gospel. Why do we look for explanations of the background? Because, on the surface, the instructions just don't fit what we know to be the true character of the Gospel.

If we had treated these few statements in the same way as we treat the sentence on teaching, we would have had millions upon millions of under age (less than sixty years) widows around the world, in churches and outside the church, being sent away cold and hungry.

Quite plainly we would never build a worldwide mountain of welfare law and prohibition based on these verses. Why? As noted above, the "plain" reading of the text just doesn't seem to match the justice inherent in the Gospel.

The point is to be aware of our limitations of understanding, and the limitations imposed by what appears to be an event within the original setting and culture. Before landing heavily on a passage, especially a passage that seems to offend the Gospel, we are compelled to allow some latitude into our thinking in case there may be circumstances we don't know about.

Life in God's world

In the introduction, I described a night, vivid in my memory, in which the rules changed. It occurred in the very strong, conservative evangelical church of my childhood, a church in which a woman in the pulpit would have been like a pork chop in a synagogue. Even a woman handling a tray of communion glasses would have been anathema. However, one day that magnificent woman, the great and powerful force for the Gospel in China, Gladys Aylward, came to our church. She was allowed to preach from behind the pulpit and did so for at least two hours to an over-packed church. We were all stunned by her testimony and the power of her ministry and message. People were deeply affected. I still remember her, the meeting and some of her exact sentences fifty years later!

Not one female member of that church would ever have been allowed to stand behind that pulpit and preach, exhort, rebuke and correct. But Gladys Aylward *was* permitted. Why did the leaders allow her to speak? Was it that, in a moment of weakness, they slid into liberalism and feminism? Or was it because it was just not possible to deny what God had done through her? In my opinion, what the male leadership discovered, at least for one night, was that their view of women just did not stand up to the realities of life in God's world.

God's ways are not our ways

Most of us recognise that, in practice, our views on the silence of women don't really work. At a local level, in many churches where women are forbidden to be a Sunday speaker, they are most welcome to offer contributions in Bible study meetings. They can contribute their answers and wisdom, and people learn from them. That is because the closer we come to God's way of doing things, the less tensions we feel, and the more things begin to slot into their correct place. (See above: Understanding the Setting)

But beyond the local level, our views seem to be even less tenable. I now spend a great deal of time teaching the Bible in regions where the Gospel has survived and grown under immense hardship. In some cases they are first-generation believers in forbidden places.

Some of the churches I have encountered are predominantly comprised of women. In some places, in recent history, every male over the age of sixteen had been rounded up and shot, or taken away to a slave-labour camp. In those churches where women are the majority, and may have been the ones who walked through the fires of persecution and loss for the sake of Christ, will we silence them as soon as a male comes to Christ? Or will we import a male speaker from hundreds of kilometres away rather than allowing the women to share the knowledge and wisdom they have gained through the fires of persecution?

Yes, those *are* (to us) exceptional circumstances. However, it is not just exceptional conditions that produce outstanding women and provide them with the opportunities for service. One of my former students, a woman, became the first missionary to her own ethnic Muslim people group. She risked a great deal, she spoke of Christ boldly and planted a church. The church has grown. The people defer to her as a leader, and learn from her knowledge and wisdom, because she is the only one with knowledge of the Bible. Shall we silence her as soon as a man comes to Christ?

My point is not to teach by example regardless of Scripture, but to say that we are living in God's world. It is *His* Kingdom, and as King, *He* does as He wishes. Our interpretations of Scripture must also fit with His activity in His world, because He will not act contrary to His character or ways. That is not an argument born of pragmatism, but a simple, honest observation.

Women in mission

Any balanced reading of the history of mission will reveal that God has used women at the forefront of opening regions for the Gospel, establishing churches in unreached areas, and ministering to men and women as they grow to maturity in Christ.

Faced with such a dilemma, the lament is often made, "Yes, but where were the men?" I find that deeply offensive! It is simply a way of saying that the only reason God used a woman was because He couldn't find an available man. That comment may well be acceptable from someone who denies the sovereignty of God over salvation and the administration of the Gospel in His world, but on the lips of someone who believes in the sovereignty of God, it is so demeaning of God as to be utterly reprehensible. It is also utterly demeaning of the women God chose to be His workers. Was Gladys Aylward nothing more than God's second best for China? What about Isobel Kuhn? Mary Slessor? Hannah Hurnard? Helen Roseveare? Rosalind Goforth?[9]

Go back to Romans 16, for example, and read through the gallery of women who were pioneers of our faith, working alongside Paul. Do we imagine that their voices were never heard?

God's chosen instrument

The result of Gladys Aylward's preaching that day in my home church when I was a young boy is still bearing fruit in my life today. It is also bearing fruit in the lives of a number of others who accepted the challenge she brought from God to take the Gospel to a lost and dying world. She taught, rebuked, corrected, and reshaped men's lives!

Why was she acceptable in the pulpit? Indeed why was her *life* acceptable? After all, in China she commanded government officials, advised governors, and stood up against official decrees; she evangelised men, taught them the Bible, advised them about their lives and families,

---

9   If you haven't heard of some of these women, it is worth chasing up a biography or two. Some of them are heroines whose courage and power are deeply humbling. And many, many men have been taught, rebuked, corrected and blessed by their writings.

and rebuked them where necessary. Was her life nothing more than a convenient disobedience condoned by God because He couldn't find any men to do it? Or was she His chosen servant, sent, commissioned and equipped by the Spirit of God for a fundamental role in the planting and watering of the Gospel in China?

Why was she acceptable when she came over here to Australia? Perhaps because she was from "over there" not here. However, whatever our theology of women, it must work "here" as well as "over there".

I dearly long to understand the Gospel fully as it applies to women as well as men. I want to understand the way God works in His world, without compromising or demeaning Him. I do not want any solution or interpretation that will compromise the Gospel or suggest that God is incapable of running His world in accordance with Scripture.

It is now time to return to the key passages in the New Testament. The exposition, or explanation, of the key passages below is an unashamed attempt to reconcile those passages with the Gospel. Please note that! It is not an exposition driven by a need to find a loophole. I am a man, I am a teacher, so frankly, I don't need any loopholes. My ego and I are well served by the compulsory submissive silence of fifty percent of the people. No, what follows is Gospel-driven. I am perplexed by any and every subject where I see a shadow cast across the brilliance of the Gospel, and to me this could be one such subject. You must judge.

Specific Bible passages

Some current interpretations

We now come to look at the specific texts related to women and the use of their voices and their spiritual gifts. Quite apart from the general injunctions for us all to teach one another, encourage one another, and for all to prophesy, there are specific gifts (charismata) and by any observation those gifts are not restricted to men. So the discussion will need to be about both the general function of women within the Body and about the use of specific gifts.

As we approach the texts, it may be helpful to state the various major views associated with the subject:

+ Women are forbidden to speak (including praying) in a meeting under any and all circumstances. (Unless, of course, the words are set to music.)
+ Women are able to "share" or give testimony but not teach.
+ Women are able to "share", and even instruct, in a living room but not from behind a pulpit.
+ Women are able to participate fully as members of the Body. However, the role of eldership is restricted to men in the same way as headship is a male role within the family.
+ Women may fulfil all roles within the Body, according to their gifts.

Beyond these, there is a plethora of views that have come about by the pharisaic addition of rules upon rules, such as:

+ Women are only to have a voice through their husbands. (You might like to work out how that is supposed to happen in real life! "Tell them this, honey; tell them that...")

- Women are not to teach, instruct, or exercise authority over any male who has reached puberty, or is over 18, or is over 21 – not even in normal "secular" life.
- Individual women are not to lead "services", including leading the singing, however they can sing as part of a *group* of song-leading women.
- Women can lead singing but not say "teachy" sorts of words between the songs.

There will be absolutely no end to this second list, because law is like that. I recall being in a major denominational church in the former Soviet Union, in which women were permitted to say poems, or to sing in the meetings. However, it was realised by some of the men that the women were occasionally using Bible verses when they introduced their songs or poems; and of course, that was teaching! So, a new decree! Women were permitted to sing but not to use a Bible verse to describe what the song was about. Rules, upon rules, upon rules. Exactitude requires more and more additions, just like our national taxation law, with its thousands of pages to cover every minute situation. That is just the way law is, and it should make us all the more grateful for the Gospel and wisdom, the two foundations of our behaviour.

The various views mentioned above derive not from a mountain of Biblical text, but from a few sentences. Let's look at those sentences.

1 Corinthians 14:33b-35

In the final section of 1 Corinthians 14, after having told the whole church to be diligent to build each other up through prophecy, and having already told the women that this was a function in which they could participate, Paul then tells women to be silent.

'Silence" means "silence" *but* "prophecy" means "prophecy". How then do we blend together chapter 11, in which women are permitted to pray and prophesy, and chapter 14 in which they are told to be silent? While it is *never* our prerogative to "get around" anything we find difficult, it *is* our responsibility to make accurate interpretations of seemingly incongruous statements in the light of the Gospel. We *must* arrive at the interpretation that best fits the Gospel.

Our primary task is to discover original intent; in this case, what was being corrected. Please note the obvious:

- It is addressed only to married women, for they alone have husbands at home.
- It is addressed only to married women with believing husbands, for unbelievers would not be able to answer their questions regarding issues discussed in church meetings.
- And it appears to be targeted at the asking of questions, or questioning.

In achieving an interpretation, we must set the words into their wider context, which we see as beginning in verse 26. The whole passage would be 26-35.

In the section beginning in verse 26 (and indeed throughout the whole chapter), we see that, in the meetings of the church, *all* are welcome to speak; "for you can all prophesy in turn" (14:31) and the others are to "weigh carefully what is said." One speaker is able to add to, or perhaps contradict, what another has said as a revelation is given by the Spirit. Another is able to take over from a speaker, having the first speaker sit down. According to the Bible, that is the way church meetings were run and directed by the Spirit of God.

In this situation, where people weigh, challenge, take over and correct, it is unbecoming for a married woman to question what her own husband is saying in the public meeting. Rather, she is to "ask her own husband at home." It appears Paul is telling us that our re-creation in Christ does not overturn the normal proprieties of marriage.

Around the table

Perhaps you have had the experience at a dinner party. No one is in the least troubled by the fact that husbands and wives both contribute to the conversation, at times adding to each other's comments. We are happy for the women to speak of the Lord at such times, and do not even blink an eyelid when husband and wife share their wisdom and knowledge or speak in praise of what God is doing in their lives. But, in such a setting, if the wife disagrees with her husband, correcting him by pointed questions or comment, what happens? Tension enters the room and we don't quite know how to cover the situation. No one knows where to look. We are embarrassed. It is better for such questioning and comments to be made privately so as not to appear to overturn God's family order.

Very few of those who hold fast to the silence of women would prevent women from asking a question in a Bible study group[10]. If a woman wanted to know something, have an answer to a perplexing problem, or even ask how she might know Christ, would any of our silence-of-women advocates refuse her the opportunity to receive help and counsel? Would they refuse to let her ask any other person, only her own husband (who might not have the answer anyway) and then only when they were physically located at home? Probably not.

My point is that, in being keen to sincerely obey this portion of Scripture as it was "plainly written", few people actually find themselves willing or able to do so, but make expedient exceptions. They select. And usually the selection is made in keeping with the innate desire for male dominance.[11]

The believers in Corinth had too much of their culture mixed with their freedom in Christ, too much self-aggrandisement and pride, resulting in chaos in their meetings. Paul has dealt with these issues. This family-order within meetings is now one more issue that God needed to clarify through Paul, and he does so in these verses.

In God's world there is order for the family. The Gospel does not overturn that order. But equally, the Gospel does not confuse the church

---

10   I realise that some do practice this complete silencing of women.
11   It is also worth noting that when Paul says they are to be "in submission", he does not say who to. To whom are women required to submit? To their husbands. Beyond that, an interesting point is that the word we have translated as "submit" is exactly the same word he used two sentences before to speak of self-control. That, by the way, is in keeping with the whole flow of the chapter – controlled use of charismata and wisdom in order to build up the church. So there is every indication that Paul is actually telling women to learn with self-control. That is what the word can mean.

and the family. Women *can* pray, they *can* prophesy, the Gospel *has* made a difference, but in weighing up what is said (14:29), and perhaps rising to speak against or correct what has been said, the married women must not question their own husbands in the meeting but must do so at home (in recognition of God's order of headship[12]).

- Does this interpretation preserve the Gospel? (This is the big question!) *Yes*, wonderfully so. Adam and Eve have now both been restored to that one-flesh position in which they both have equal access to, and acceptance by, God.

- Does this interpretation preserve God's order for marriage? *Yes*. Eve's submission is seen in her loving restraint. She will preserve the dignity of Adam and ask him at home. She will not humiliate him. Nor will he demean her.

- Does this interpretation preserve the concept of the Body, fully gifted and fully responsible for mutual ministry? *Yes*. Women, as part of the Body, can share their wisdom and knowledge in prayer and prophecy.

- Does this interpretation preserve the Corinthian responsibilities of *all* bringing something to the meeting, *all* prophesying, *all* having a hymn or word from God ready and available for mutual edification? *Yes* again.

- Is this interpretation practical for the life and ministry of the Body in all cultures, in all political, racial circumstances, especially where the church is mostly comprised of women, or churches where there are only "baby" men? *Yes*.

---

12 Here and elsewhere, I am working in harmony with the traditional view of headship within the family. However, the exact implications and application of the term "head" must also be removed from the innate desire of men to rule, and reviewed on the basis of the Gospel and the original intentions of God for husbands and wives. To make the term "submission", when applied to wives, to be of greater consequence than the model of the absolute sacrifice of Christ as applied to husbands, is an imbalance unworthy of men renewed in Christ. (Ephesians 5:21 and 25)

1 Timothy 2:11-15

We now return to what is perhaps the most blunt statement.

"I do not permit a woman to teach or have authority over a man." (1 Timothy 2:12)

As indicated in the introduction, it is worthy of note that the word "woman" here is a word that can be legitimately translated "wife" and the word "man" is a word that can be accurately translated as "husband". As we noted, both are translated that way in many, many portions of Scripture.

So how do we decide? Obviously context will be a major factor in establishing an interpretation.

The text in context

In the verses supporting that instruction, we see reference to Adam and Eve. In our terminology, they were a married couple, not just two young adults of different gender. They were the original "one flesh" couple. We also have that strange statement about women being saved through childbirth. Difficult though the statement may be to interpret, let's at least acknowledge that, in Scripture, childbirth is a marriage-related event.

In verse 11 Paul says that the "woman" should "learn in full submission."[13] (Let's take the word as submission, but we should note that Paul uses it a few sentences earlier to mean "self-control".)

The question again is: To whom is a woman to submit? To

a. all men in general,

b. all believing men, or

c. to her husband?

In the New Testament, what *is* the normal direction and application of this concept of submission when related to women? We have dealt

---

13   The whole subject of submission is a subject on its own. I am using the words here as they are traditionally used and understood, and am not implying any specific teaching or instruction or view about "submission". However, much of our understanding on this wider subject also needs to be reviewed.

with this earlier, but submission between the man and the woman, however you might see that enacted, is a family issue. All women are not subject to all men, in or out of a church meeting. My wife is not subject to every other man in the church! Such a situation would be utterly intolerable. And as her husband, I will not permit it! In the meeting it is *our* relationship that must be preserved and demonstrated, not a gender-based submission to all other men.[14]

Because of this and the other strong marriage flavours in the few verses surrounding 1 Timothy 2:12, might it not be reasonable to actually translate the words as "wife" and "husband" rather than the generic terms "woman" and "man"? If we do translate the words as "wife" and "husband", a perfectly legitimate translation of the two Greek words, and one quite appropriate to the context, we see an instruction that does not contradict the responsibility of women to prophesy and contribute to the life of the Body. We also see an instruction that, like Corinthians, maintains Biblical headship *in the family*. Most importantly, we do not see a contradiction of the Gospel, through which:

> Even on my servants, *both men and women*, I will pour out my Spirit in those days, and *they* will prophesy.

Some suggest that Paul's instruction in verse 8 about men praying applies to all men generically, and women dressing modestly applies to all women generically. Therefore, they might say, the words in verse 11 must also be directed to all men and women not to husbands and wives. That is not a line of thinking that should be dismissed lightly. However, without wishing to minimise that perspective, those verses work just as well if the words are translated husbands and wives in each case. Husbands should pray with holy hands and not in anger, and wives

---

14   As noted earlier, it is important for men to recognise that our thinking is inherited from our culture, and our culture comes from this side of the Fall. We are now in Christ, and we will be different from Islam, from Hinduism, and from all cultures around the world where men rule over women as slaves, chattels and lesser beings. And as you read in Genesis that the woman was made as a "helper" for the man, just remember what was noted earlier: that in many portions of Scripture, God is described as our "helper" using exactly the same word. And God is most definitely not made inferior to us by the use of that word!

should dress as godly women. (Many men express their greatest anger secretly, in the family, even to the point of beating their wives. Publicly pious, but secretly seething with anger.)

Other considerations in 1 Timothy

It is also worth noting that the letter of 1 Timothy presupposes some serious problems, some of which remain only vague for us. As you read through the letter, you will easily see that there was the teaching of false doctrines, myths and endless genealogies (1:3-4). As a result, some had wandered away from the faith.

You will also see that two members, Alexander and Hymenaeus have been "delivered to Satan". Men (or husbands) are urged to pray without disputing and to step away from anger. Timothy is warned about those who follow deceiving spirits, those who forbid marriage, those with utterly corrupted consciences. There are godless myths and "old wives tales" in the church. As we noted earlier, there was some sort of order of widows to which they pledged their devotion, but some of the young widows were breaking their pledges by remarrying. Others were becoming busybodies and idle gossipers. There was "envy, strife, malicious talk, evil suspicions and the constant friction between men of corrupt minds." Men were preaching for financial gain, a terrible corruption of the use of God-given gifts in ministry.

This was anything but a peaceful church in which godliness was the order of the day! It was a church that was corrupted in many ways.

Is it possible that within that church there was also a corruption of the family roles, and the women were dominating the men? Is it possible that the women were among those "who want to be teachers of the law but they do not know what they are talking about or what they so confidently affirm"? (1:7) Was it that the women *were* in fact behaving like Eve, and became the first ones to listen to the false teachers, swayed as Eve was when she listened to Satan? In other words, was Paul addressing a *specific* situation in a chaotic church, or was he laying down

31

a rule that countermands what he said to the Corinthians and what God promised with the coming of the Spirit? (Acts 2:17-18)

I think that something specific *is* happening here. The concept of Eve being deceived and therefore all women throughout all history are more susceptible to deception does not easily withstand the scrutiny of history. Men are equally capable of being deceived by Satan, as evidenced by the fact that, in many countries, more women are believers than men, i.e. women have accepted the truth while men are still deceived. If Paul is addressing a *specific* situation, he is illustrating it with a specific parallel from the *Fall*, not from creation. Our Gospel behaviour is not, and *never should be*, determined by the Fall. It should be determined by the original creation and subsequent re-creation in Christ.

Paul's creation-based illustration

What lies behind Paul's illustration is that, in the garden, the man, who was created first, had the word of God given to him *directly*. Therefore he knew *directly* and should not have embraced his wife's acceptance of Satan's corruption of that word. His wife, who did *not* have the word of God directly (see the order of events in Genesis 2) should not have presumed to know, she should have asked her husband. That is the event to which Paul is pointing, and that is how creation and deception blend together in the illustration Paul gives.

Whatever the specific situation being addressed, these comments by Paul concerning the church at Ephesus are not set within a quiet discussion of order in the church aimed at refining what was already good and godly practise. These comments are written into a situation of near chaos. To build a mountain of prohibition gagging fifty percent of all believers, or as some do, fifty percent of the whole population of the world, for all of human history based on this sentence, is building on a weak foundation, *especially* when there is a very legitimate dispute over the intended meaning of the words wife/woman, husband/man. And equally so when that mountain of prohibition goes against the clear promise of the coming of the Spirit in which God would deliberately overturn Jewish and Gentile social order by the emancipation of women and their freedom to prophesy, which cannot be done without speaking.

As noted above, we do not give the same weight to other portions of the same letter (like the issue of the widows). Why? At the worst it might be because we are men who innately want to rule over women, and this sentence on teaching enables us to do it with a pure religious motive and Biblical backing.

Charles Williams' translation, which many suggest gives full weight to the Greek idiom as well as grammar, renders verse 11,

> I do not permit a married woman to practise teaching or domineering over a husband.[15]

If Williams is correct, we suddenly have a massive new potential for the dissemination of truth and building up of the saints because the other fifty percent can now share their God-given wisdom and use their God-given gifts.

A conclusive argument?

So is the wife/husband argument conclusive? Not based on the sentence itself, because it can equally be translated woman/man. So why would God allow something as important as the gagging of fifty percent of the population of believers for two thousand years, to rest on a few words of double meaning written into a social setting that is no longer clear to us? Let me suggest that *we* are the ones who have made it a major issue, not God. *We* are the ones who have made it an issue of ranking supremacy, upon which name-calling and division are based and even orthodoxy assessed. *We* are the ones who have enabled that sentence to perpetuate the oppression that the unbelieving, pagan world has perpetrated for all of the millennia since the Fall. Perhaps that was never God's intention, and that the issue is not one that stands or falls on a sentence, but one that

---

15   C B Williams, The New Testament In the Language Of the People. (Nashville, 1986) But note that this is not universally accepted as a rendering. Our view of a translation of this verse will usually be coloured by our predetermined view of the subject.

stands or falls on the Gospel. And, as indicated above, the Gospel always has been the great leveller, raising women up and bringing men down to the same level. In Christ, the redemption of women has always been complete and never did contain a lingering impediment to the exercise of gifts and the sharing of wisdom. Our arguments over a sentence or two, and conclusions which undermine the realities of the Gospel, are arguments that are born of the age old Eden struggle, indicating that we have not yet been transformed by the full and complete renewing of our minds.

If I might use Gladys Aylward as an example once again, imagine sitting in a room in China with some men who are young in Christ, and in one corner, with a Bible open in her lap, sits a small woman. From her lips come wisdom as, night after night, the men drink from the living waters that flow from within her. In that totally male-dominant culture, God chose a woman – a very small woman – to shame the prevailing wisdom and to demonstrate the brilliance of His wisdom in Christ. He showed them that in Christ there is neither male nor female, that what their male-dominated culture considered weak and foolish was indeed a repository of His divine wisdom and power.

If it was within your power, would you silence this "small woman"?

Female elders

So what about female elders? Does the passage in Timothy, or any other passage forbid that? I am sure there will be honest disagreement about that. However, remember that the verse does not say that. Please note that fact. It does *not* say that women cannot be elders. That is an interpretative application, and one that perhaps does not adequately support the enormous weight of law, wrath and division which the one single word "authority" has created. This is especially true in the light of the equally valid translation, "wife...husband." If an adequate and quite reasonable translation of Paul's words is as Williams suggests (quoted above), then the phrase as a foundation for centuries of restrictive male domination over gifted and wise female believers all but crumbles to dust. It must be noted, however, that the qualifications for eldership in a local church, as set out in Timothy and Titus, are male. While that may be consistent with the generic cultural use of the male gender in speaking of the wider body (e.g. "all men are saved..." meaning "all people"), eldership being exclusively male is a position that carries considerable weight.

However, can I say to the women that, if I was not permitted to be an elder but was allowed to fully use my gifts in any and every other way, and saw fruit for my labours, I really wouldn't be too concerned if that office was denied me. A little frustrated perhaps, I am not sure, but not even angry enough to kick the cat. Most *men* are in *exactly* that position.

In thinking through and debating the eldership issue, remember again to get the setting right. Biblical leadership is eldership, and that is always plural. The concept of one pastor in charge of a church is not a role that can be found or defended in or through any portion of the New Testament.[16]

The New Testament leadership setting of a group of godly elders caring for the Lord's people as servants is neither a titled nor elevated position. As such, it may be less egotistically desirable for men as well as women than is our current model of elevated, titled, salary-guaranteed pastors.

What these passages do not say

These two passages, Corinthians and Timothy, do not say that
+ Women were created inferior
+ All men must rule over all women
+ Any man must rule over any woman
+ Women can only speak through their husbands
+ The cut-off point for women to give direction to males, or share their wisdom and knowledge with them, is male puberty

---

16   I realise that is a bold statement in the face of such an entrenched system, but if it prompts you to study the subject, well and good. You may find that the noun "pastor" is used only once in the whole New Testament, whereas the noun "elder" is used 21 times. In your study, check the use of the words pastor, elder and bishop in the Greek, using a Strongs Concordance or some such tool. Look at how they are used, of whom, and in what setting. Look at what their roles are. For more on this, see THE GATHERING, Littleman Publishing.

- Musical accompaniment makes the difference as to whether women can be heard or not
- Women cannot speak to men even in a secular setting
- In Eden, Eve was to keep quiet
- Women are not saved from Eve's deception

Or any one of a hundred little rules and extrapolations! These are rules not interpretations. They do not come within a bull's roar of what might be considered an interpretation; they are *additions* to what the Scripture says, added (usually by men) by way of intended clarification or qualification. They are not from the text but are someone's application of the text.

As you interpret any subject, ask God for wisdom to know when the Pharisee in you is adding rules to rules upon rules. Stick with the text in its varied contexts (literary, historical, cultural), and allow the ultimate context to be the Gospel.

Understanding what happens when we teach

As Graham Cole points out[17],

> "...authority comes from God and his Word and not in any part from the sex of the preacher."

It is a telling point. Explaining what something means is not an act of authority or a usurping of a role. If my wife knows more about cooking something than I do, I ask her how to do it. If my wife knows more about the application of some portions of Scripture than I do (and she does!) then I ask her. Explaining is not dominating!

Nor is the sharing of wisdom. Is the wisdom of fifty percent of the Body to be denied to the Body? Can the whole right hand side of the Body say of the whole left hand side of the Body "I have no need of you"? My wife has known Christ for forty years, has done more formal study than I have, and has ministered the counsel and wisdom of God to men and women in times of need and personal crisis in some of the world's more difficult places. Are we men saying of such women, "We will not listen to

---

17   (Women Teaching Men The Bible: What's the Problem; BriefCACE #34, September 2006)

you; we have no need of your wisdom; if you do have something to tell us, tell your husband 'non-authoritatively' and he can pass it on to us"?

Let's make sure that what we do believe does indeed work in God's world. Let's make sure that it does agree with the apportioning of gifts and wisdom by the Spirit, and that, whatever our viewpoint, it does demonstrate a complete Gospel for both men and women.

Transformed by the Gospel

We have seen that some of the key "gender texts" are open to translation and contextual questions. Paul kept his "teaching and authority" instructions within family, where submission was the rule for male-female relationships. It is our translators' choice to use the generic words "man" and "woman" rather than the words "husband" and "wife". As we saw, it is not the rule of Scripture that all women are to be subject to all men. Those instructions were family based.

In doing this we have regarded the various passages of Scripture as representing a static rule transcending time and culture. That is, we have said that in their original setting they are addressing family submission issues, and the conclusions we draw apply to all societies at all times.

But there is a further dimension to the way we work with Scripture, one that affects our manner of interpreting a number of subjects. It is one that demands, at the very least, a re-examination of our interpretive and thought processes, and at the very most, a re-examination of the way we allow Scripture to frame and shape our responses to life in God's world.

The first century family, like the society that enclosed it, was intensely patriarchal. Men ruled. Men had rights. Women were possessions. Women had no rights. New Testament instructions were written into that social milieu. The question is, "Is that God's permanent ideal for men and women?"

The question is best understood by examining a universally accepted parallel example.

* * *

In the early 1800s, the movement to abolish slavery in Britain and America was approaching its peak. Many of those who promoted the maintenance of slavery did so on Biblical grounds. They said, quite correctly, that the Bible did not outlaw slavery, but, to the contrary, condoned slavery by giving explicit instructions about how slaves and masters should operate. Slaves were to submit to their masters, and the masters were to treat their slaves well. But slaves remained slaves and masters remained masters.

A slave was the property of his or her master, and in no place in Scripture are believers told to fight against the concept of a man or woman being owned by another.

The pro-slavery lobby would have suggested that the abolitionists were acting contrary to the written words of Scripture. God explicitly said, "Slaves submit…masters treat fairly". God nowhere said, "Masters set your slaves free" or "slaves run from your masters."

However, as evangelical believers, we hail as heroes of the faith those men and women who fought tirelessly for abolition. It is something we feel intuitively from the Gospel of grace and freedom; and also from what men and women were created to be. Although not explicitly stated in the creation account, we see in that account, that men and women were created free and were given a mandate to work in freedom and dignity before God.

So on what basis do we applaud abolition? By what right do we applaud the abolitionists who sought to improve upon Scripture?

In upholding abolition, we are acknowledging that, in the first-century, the social institution of slavery existed, and within that social structure, God established patterns for Christian behaviour. However, the first-century existence of slavery does not mean that slavery is God's permanent, social ideal. It is how society was, and within that social structure, slaves and masters had to act with godliness.

We naturally locate the slavery texts within their first-century cultural milieu but go beyond scripture in our own application, because we have had the ability and opportunity to change those social structures.

God has also said "Wives submit...husbands love." This was also spoken into an oppressive social situation in which the women were possessions of the men, and all gender rights belonged to the man. (As we saw, this came from the Fall, not from creation.) The husband had commanding authority in the marriage, and he alone had the power to terminate it. Women had no social power.

That is the social structure that existed, and within that structure, men and women had to act with godliness. Paul did not overthrow the intensely patriarchal structures of the time. Perhaps to do so would have left many women vulnerable, just as overthrowing slavery would have left many without work, shelter or food. But does that mean that the prevailing gender structures of the time were God's permanent, social ideal?

My point is not to flesh out that whole slavery-gender comparison[18], but to test our thinking as to why it is so easy to be adamant about patriarchal rule when, on slavery, scripture uses the same "submission" words. And regarding slavery, we would fight vehemently for the right of men and women to be free *despite* what the texts explicitly say.

Is it possible that, *just as happened with slavery*, while God corrected the prevailing first-century gender abuses, God never intended for those corrective words to be seen as his permanent, highest social ideal for men and women, husbands and wives?

If we are honest about an even-handed method of interpretation and application, then yes – it must at least be *possible*. We must, at least, think it through.

God redeemed the social structures of the slavery that existed at the time, but we went further and set slaves fully free. We did so on the basis of the principles of the equal value of men and women inherent in the Gospel and the created order. God also redeemed the gender structures that were in place. Why would we not set women fully free on those same principles inherent in that same Gospel and created order?

---

18   If you wish to do some thoughtful reading on the subject, I highly recommend *Slaves, Women and Homosexuals: Exploring the Hermeneutics of Cultural Analysis* by William J. Webb, IVP, Downers Grove, 2001. I am very much indebted to Webb for his contribution to Biblical hermeneutics.

It is important for both sides of the women-in-Christ debate to do the personal soul-searching, looking for the foundations of our "righteous indignation", as well as doing the serious hermeneutical (interpretation) exercises.

Not only slavery

Other examples of this type of movement to a higher ideal can readily be found. We value our participation in democracy, using our freedom to vote against the ruler of the day and to turn him or her out of office. It is hardly obeying the rule of Scripture to "honour" those in authority by turning them out of office.

On this issue, we have allowed progressive movement in our practise, based on the fact that we are now in a different society – we are free and educated, and free, educated people need to be free to think and to exercise their wisdom concerning the running of their nation.

Similarly, we have changed the Biblical laws of inheritance, preferring to preserve the right to give all siblings, male and female, the same inheritance if we wish. We have outlawed the Biblically accepted practise of polygamy despite numerous Biblical examples and the absence of any condemnation of it. (Apart from the description of the required marital status of church elders.)

A principle of interpretation

What happens is that, as society changes, and vulnerabilities are removed, we continue to "improve" upon Biblical norms by working in the same creation/Gospel direction as Scripture. We are not going against God's wishes, but are working in the same direction. We are being "transformed by the renewing of our minds."

The principle, simply stated, is one of seeing God redeeming the cultures of the day[19], while ultimately moving his people towards his ideal.

---

19   Webb (see footnote 1) has applied the term "redemptive-movement hermeneutic" to describe the observable process of God changing, or redeeming, the culture of the day, and thus indicating to his people a movement towards the "ultimate ethic".

We see *some* Old Testament slavery and gender laws[20] as utterly abhorrent, and would want them outlawed in any and every society today. However, in their day and culture, they were shockingly progressive. So, too, were New Testament instructions shockingly progressive. On the slavery issue, we do not generally see them as progressive enough. *Perhaps* other considerations apply, but the question must the addressed: Is *any* movement possible or necessary on the gender issues?

Are we saying that God changes his mind on issues? No, but even a casual comparison of the Old and New Testaments shows that he clearly changes the level of application of his desires, according to the ability of the culture of the day to absorb it. (As a parent my goal was the safety of my children. That never changed. But along the way I broadened what they were permitted to do, because as they matured, their abilities and wisdom changed.)

Between the Old and New Testaments, God dramatically changed the application of his desires regarding slavery and women. On slavery, we have gone further. And, now that women are not the possessions of men in an oppressively patriarchal society, what shall we say about women in Christ?

---

20   If you have never read them, it would be worth doing. For example, beating a slave almost to death is acceptable, as long as he can get out of bed in a couple of days. Sexually abusing a slave girl is not as serious as sexually abusing a free woman. A woman can be taken as one of the spoils of war. If you rape a woman you must pay her father some money and marry the girl – whether she likes it or not. No reparation needs to be made to the woman.

A final word

Ladies, this is not a war.

Men, this is not a coup.

If the subject is approached in any way that resembles the gender struggle established at the Fall, we will never begin to grasp the wisdom of God. If one side wishes to usurp and the other to dominate, we do not have the heart attitude necessary to discover the Truth of God's ways.

The discussion should be an honest attempt by men and women of the Gospel to find the correct application of the Gospel to both men and women. If the Gospel gives men freedom from their past and Adam's past, it should give women freedom from their past and Eve's past. If the Gospel lifts men up to "the glorious liberty" of being sons of God, it should equally lift women to glorious liberty.

It is the application of our emancipation in Christ that is under discussion. It is the extent to which the Gospel has dealt with broken humanity. Unfortunately too little of the Gospel has been injected into the arguments that have arisen over recent decades.

If we have differences of opinion, we still ought to be on "the same side of the table." We are not enemies approaching an issue on which we hope to win, but servants of Christ who want His ways to win in us and in those with whom we are linked by the one Spirit. It is not a matter of politics and power plays, but of discerning and applying true Gospel-based wisdom.

It was not long ago that, even in our post-Reformation society, women were not allowed to vote, not allowed to receive higher education, to be doctors or pursue any other type of profession. For women to write books was a scandal, for them to have an opinion was thought ludicrous.

They were to sit in intellectual suffocation doing needlepoint, only to be bargained off in marriage to the advantage of the parents. Some of this was within our grandparents' lifetimes!

And the church happily complied with these sad evidences of the curse, able to do it from a "godly" motive. In recent years, women have come a long way but, sadly, it has often been a secular world that has exposed our prejudices and dragged believers into seasons of change. This ensured that the issue was radicalised by giving the discussion into the hands of those with a political agenda, not a Gospel agenda.

As we continue to think through this subject, we need to make it our priority to discover the truth, and then to speak the truth *in love*. Women must also be free to speak the truth in the discussion. After all, it is their lives we are discussing!

And ladies, you *must* speak the truth. Just as it is all too easy and comfortable for men to sit in arrogant pre-eminence, so too is it all too comfortable for many women to sit in docile passivity. If there is a role for you to play within the Kingdom, and if God has given you the spiritual gifts to fulfil that role, then you have no choice but to walk in His ways. The gifts come at a price and the price is responsibility.

Along the way, "Make every effort to keep the unity of the Spirit through the bond of peace." Ephesians 4:3

For conversation

These questions are intended to give you something to talk about, a focus for beginning your conversation. Allow them to challenge your own thoughts, feelings and attitudes. The questions do not presume that this booklet is correct in all its conclusions, they presume only that the subject does give is something to talk about. Start anywhere, and wander wherever you wish.

1. On page 34 there is a brief comment on Gladys Aylward, and the question is posed: "If it was within your power would you silence this small woman?" Discuss this honestly as you reflect on your views. To this you might add the question: "If Gladys Aylward was doing this in your church – a woman preaching, teaching, rebuking, exhorting men, leading them to Christ and then to maturity – would the church silence her?" Why or why not?

   (If you are unfamiliar with Gladys Aylward, by all means extend your conversation to Dr Helen Roseveare, [missionary to Congo and author] Corrie ten Boom [whose books have changed the lives of men and women], Evangeline Booth [daughter of William Booth], Elisabeth Elliot, Isobel Kuhn *or any one else* who comes to mind.)

2. Discuss the "boundary" of submission mentioned on page 15. Have you been given the impression that, within the church, all women are to submit to all men? Is it stated or implied? Do you feel that that is a creation-based concept? Or is it culturally derived?

3. In the section "The Gospel and women", beginning on page 4, the underlying question is, "What does redemption mean for women?" Discuss this fully and openly. Trite answers won't help, nor will heated arguments! Really think it through, and as you do, continue to refer to relevant Bible passages.

4. Examine Paul's use of the Greek word for woman/wife and man/husband. Read the following verses in which these words are used and make your observations. Discuss your observations in general, and then specifically in regard to 1 Timothy 2:9-15.

a) Woman/wife
   1 Corinthians 11:3,5-13,15; 14:34,35
   Galatians 4:4
   Ephesians 5:22-25,28,31,33
   Colossians 3:18,19
   1 Timothy 2:9-12,14; 3:2,11,12; 5:9
   Titus 1:6
b) Man/husband
   Romans 4:8; 7:2,3; 11:4
   1 Corinthians 7:2-4,10,11,13,14,16,34,39; 11:3,4,7-9,11,12,14; 13:11; 14:35
   2 Corinthians 11:2
   Galatians 4:27
   Ephesians 4:13; 5:22-25,28,33
   Colossians 3:18,19
   1 Timothy 2:8,12; 3:2,12; 5:9; Tit 1:6; 2:5

   (It is a huge exercise, but to be really thorough, using a Strongs Concordance in print or in your computer, you could go right through the whole NT. However, Paul's use is probably sufficient at this time.)

5. As you approach this subject, how much has your own (personal) perspective been shaped by the Fall, how much has been shaped by Creation, and how much has been shaped by the Gospel? Try and identify the various components of your own thinking.

6. In some quarters it is said, "A woman's true fulfilment and purpose is in marrying and having children." Do history, or life in God's world, make a comment on this?

7. In what ways do you feel the various "silence" views (examples are on pages 24 and 25) reflect on the subject of the redemption of women? Are the two issues – speaking and redemption – connected or disconnected?

8. If women were no longer silent, what would it mean in practical terms in the life of local churches? How would *you* construct local church life?

9. *Suggestion*: As a group exercise, get hold of a book like The Small Woman by Alan Burgess, or the biography of any other woman missionary who interests you, and read it as a group. Then discuss what you learn about God and His ways. Imagine whichever missionary you have chosen working in your district. What would she be allowed and not allowed to do?

Also by Ray Barnett

The
Gathering

Rediscovering the simplicity, power and effectiveness of
God's first-century pattern for the church

Why is the institutional church such a frustrating, ineffective
experience for so many sincere believers?

Why do we seem to repel the very people that Jesus attracted?
Why is it, that for all the dollars spent on buildings, clergy salaries,
and denominational hierarchies, the institutional church seems to
remain so ineffective and powerless to change our communities, let
alone genuinely impact our own lives?

The simple answer is that, for too many centuries, our institutional
structures have been based on a lie. We have been 'sold' the notion
that the leadership hierarchies, the clergy system, and the auditorium-
based cycles of Sunday meetings are what God instructs us to do in
Scripture.

Nothing could be further from the truth.

The Gathering challenges each of those institutional fallacies in a
detailed re-examination of what God actually does say about being a
local church. For believers who are walking away from the suffocations
of the past, or who would like to, The Gathering lays out a pathway
towards a truer, more Biblical model of the local church.

Published by Littleman Publishing

www.ingramcontent.com/pod-product-compliance
Lightning Source LLC
Chambersburg PA
CBHW021226020426
42331CB00003B/488